About the Book

Adobe Photoshop and Lightroom are two of the most widely used photo editing software in the world. They are used by a wide variety of people including photographers, both professional and amateur, graphic designers and even 3D artists.

Adobe Photoshop in particular, has perhaps the most applications and is the most versatile photo processing and manipulation software.

This book will introduce to you some of the fundamentals of Adobe Photoshop, as well as teach you the basic and intermediate level editing techniques. You will learn how to use Photoshop to edit your photos in specific ways, impose several different effects, and retouch your image like a professional.

You will also learn how to edit and process Raw image files on Photoshop, as well as the basics of the Raw format.

It is important to note that while this book gives tutorials on how to implement specific effects and filters, depending on the software version you are using, some of the options mentioned and discussed in this book may not be present. In such a case, it is advised to install a more recent version of Photoshop that has all of the effects and options available as standard.

Contents

Introduction

Adobe Photoshop is hailed as a necessity, a must-have, for any professional photographer, as well as anyone with a digital camera and the desire to manipulate or edit their photos according to their liking.

The software started out for that very purpose. Today, it has become the single most versatile and expansive photo editing software in the world. It is being used by a range of individuals, across an even bigger range of applications and has emerged as the ideal solution for anyone who wishes to retouch a photo.

However, with that versatility comes an increasingly complicated and extensive list of things you can do to a photo. In the past, all you could do was crop a picture or re-align it or at most, adjust the layers or transform an image. Today, you have the capability of radically manipulating and modifying an image, vector graphics, and even to a limited extent, videos.

Following are some of the capabilities of Photoshop that you can take advantage of.

- Polish an image to your liking, and add that touch of perfection.
- Create an image using both live imagery and graphics, and come up with a masterpiece.
- Edit your image using a vast array of filters and adjustment options.
- Move or replace the objects within your image, in order to achieve a better composition.
- Combine 2 or more photos to create superimposed images.
- Transform an ordinary image into a veritable work of art.

In addition to that, you have the Adobe Camera Raw, which is now available as a filter, instead of simply being a format, and later, a tool for reading and retouching raw image files.

The immense potential for creativity brings with it complication, thus increasing the need for a guide for people who wish to explore the possibilities of photo editing.

Following is just such a guide. This guide has been constructed, keeping in mind both the beginner as well as the intermediate level photographer. There are even some tips for the advanced professional who wishes to add that extra edge to their editing.

So without further ado, let's look at what you as a photographer can do with Adobe Photoshop, and how you can improve you editing as well as photography skills.

Photoshop Basics: Understanding the Fundamentals of Photoshop

As you must already know, Photoshop is probably the single most versatile photo editing software available. Part of the popularity of Photoshop comes from the fact that almost everybody can use it, from an entry level photographer to an advanced illustrator or graphic designer.

However, in order to start working on the amazing software, you will need to first understand the fundamentals. This guide will introduce to you just some of the capabilities of Photoshop. These specific tools and applications are the most frequently used and they comprise of a set of skills that everybody at the starting level should know.

For the first time user, the interface may be a little intimidating. The software itself has evolved over the years and the current versions present a very professional looking suite, something that often confuses new users. There are now more options and applications of the software than ever, with new plug-ins and add-ons arriving on an almost weekly basis.

Simply put, understanding the software from scratch is the only option, if you hope to keep up with the developments in the future. And in order to better understand the software from scratch, first you will need to know its interface.

The Modern Photoshop Interface

Due to the rapid development of Photoshop throughout the years, the name of the software has gone through some changes. Photoshop CC is the most recent version, which is also the version that we will be discussing.

If you have an older version of the soft ware installed on to your PC, you will need to purchase the newest version, with the highest number of application.

Let us first look at the interface.

List of Basic Tools

The list of tools in Photoshop is ever expanding. Starting from just a few to the dozens that we have today, the number is expected to go up. The basic tools though, have remained a staple on the software's toolbox, partly due to their practicality and usefulness, and partly because of the way these can modify and completely transform an image.

There are several tools that define Photoshop and its functionality, chief among which are the three most used; the **Crop** tool, the **Rotating** tool and the **Resizing** tool. Slightly more advanced is the **Dodge** and **Burn** tool, which will be discussed later on in the book. Let us look at the **Crop** tool first.

Using the Crop Tool

Cropping, or removing certain parts or sections of an image, is the very first thing that comes to mind whenever we mention Photoshop. The technique of taking portions of the image, and either inserting them into another image, or removing them altogether, is also one of the first photo editing and manipulation techniques that are taught in editing classes.

Cropping an image on screen is quite similar to using a scissor for a similar purpose, on a printed photo. And with the potential for minute accuracy in the more recent versions of Photoshop, cropping can make cuts that are accurate to the pixel.

The technique of cropping, although it verbally referring to the **Crop** tool, can actually be performed in 2 ways; either by using the **Crop** tool itself, or another tool, known as Rectangular Marquee. The latter tool makes use of selection, while the former is more direct.

Following are the steps for using the standard **Crop** tool:

1. The **Tools** panel should be on the left side of the screen. Click on the **Crop** tool on the panel.
2. Visualize the portion of the image that you are going to keep, then drag the box to select the preferred part of the image. Here you will have the option to correct or modify the cropping handles. This is a slightly more advanced step and unnecessary here.
3. Both double-clicking and pressing **Enter** on the image will result in the image being cropped.

Now for the **Rectangular Marquee** tool, which you can find in the **Tools** panel as well:

1. Having selected the Rectangular Marquee tool, find the **Mode** or **Style** (depending on your version of Photoshop). It will be a drop-down type of menu.
2. Here you will have the choice to set a certain **Aspect Ratio**. Again, this is a slightly more advanced option. For now, set the Mode or Style to **Normal**.
3. Repeat the same drag and release action that was used with the **Crop** tool.
4. After you have selected the portion of the photo that you wish to keep, from the top panel, select **Image**, to open the drop-down menu.
5. From the menu, select **Crop**. The image will be similarly cropped.

Note: Cropped images usually have less detail than the original images. This is due to the size adjustment that is done to fit the picture on to the screen, while the reduced resolution results in blown-up pixels, reducing the quality of the image.

Now let's take a look at how to **Rotate** and **Resize** images:

Rotating an Image

The rotation option allows you to rotate your image both clockwise and anti-clockwise. You can also flip an image both vertically and horizontally, as well as rotate a selected image by a specific amount.

To rotate an image, use the following steps.

1. Select the **Image** option from the top panel to access the drop-down menu.
2. From the menu, select the **Image Rotation** option.
3. You will be given multiple rotation options. Select the one which looks best to you. The Image will then be rotated according to your chosen option.

To round off the basic image retouching techniques, let's look at **Resizing** images.

Resizing an Image

As mentioned earlier, increasing the size of the image reduces the amount of fine detail in the photo. However, in case you do need to resize an image, you can follow the steps given below.

1. From the top panel, select the **Image** option, to open the drop-down menu.
2. Select the **Image Size** option. This will open a dialog box.
3. Inside the dialog box set the **Pixels** options to the already set **Unit Size**.
4. The **Resample** box should be checked, and the icon named **Lock** should be on. You can find the **Lock** button beside the height and width options. This is done to make sure that the aspect ratio doesn't change, which could potentially distort the image.
5. Put in your preferred dimensions to resize the image. Entering the width of the image will enable the previous setting to come into action, adjusting the aspect ratio accordingly.
6. When you have adjusted the width and height according to your liking, select **OK** at the bottom of the dialog box. This will resize the image.

These are the basic tools and techniques that will let you get a feel for how the software works, while also giving you an idea about what else you can do with an image. However, in order to regularly edit your images, you must know how to quickly load, and after you are done editing, save your edited images.

Loading Images

If you are using Photoshop for the purpose of editing images, you will be selecting your file from a list of existing images. Your selected file can be of a wide range of formats including but not limited to JPG, PNG, PSD (Photoshop document) or camera-specific formats such as NEF(Nikon Electronic Format).

To load an image on to the editing screen, follow the steps given below.

1. From the top panel, select the **File** option.
2. Next, click on **Open**. This will open a dialog box.
3. The dialog box should automatically open the relevant folder (the one containing the bulk of the images, or the system generated image folder).
4. Click on the image you wish to edit and press **Open**, at the bottom of the dialog box.

Let's move on to saving an edited image.

Saving an Image

When you have finished editing a photo, you will have several options regarding the format in which you wish to save the image. The most common formats are JPEG and PNG however a variety of other formats can be used as well. Some of them are explained below.

Photoshop Documents (PSD)

This is the format that the edited images are saved in, by default. This specific format is different from the simpler formats in the way that it actually saves all the editing data along with the image itself. This means that the images that you have edited once can be modified again and again, with all the layers and miscellaneous modifications saved as they are.

One drawback of this file format is that is made specifically for Photoshop. This means that you can only open the image that you have saved in this format, or an image that you have received in this format, in Photoshop only. If you wish to share images with someone who doesn't have Photoshop, you will need to either save the photo in a simpler format in the first place, or convert it before sending.

Save For Web: This is not as much a format as it is a convenience feature. Save For Web is used primarily for optimizing photos, to facilitate online uploading. The photos are compressed as much as possible while retaining much of the image quality. Save for Web also allows users to resize and adjust images which are then prepared for uploading. The photos that are uploaded using this feature are also much smaller in size, as compared to JPEG and especially RAW images.

Getting to Know Layers

More often than not, the first thing that comes to mind when you think of Photoshop are the brilliantly extravagant imagery and heavily edited photos. A simple picture with minimal effects and effort behind it can be made into an artistic masterpiece, and a bright and upbeat picture can have graphics and various other fantastic effects on it.

While there are several ways and techniques that can be used for such photo manipulation, the tool that is the most frequently used for this purpose is **Layers**.

Layers are perhaps the single most important as well as useful tool in any photographer's arsenal, as far as photo editing is concerned. For anyone who would like to achieve any level of expertise at Photoshop, the **Layers** tool can open up a world of editing possibilities.

To better understand the tool and all that it encompasses, we will be breaking it down into the two types of Layers that are available; namely **Content Layers** and **Adjustment Layers**.

Content Layers

These layers can contain a wide variety of content, hence the name. Content here refers to shapes, text, photos etc. The number of options available to users is astounding, and you can even download custom content that other creators have made, which makes it a very flexible tool as well.

Content layers make up the bulk of the **Layers** tool. When you engage a content layer, you are adding 'content' to the photo, and the more content you add, the more layers you will have, one on top of the other.

Adjustment Layers

These are the layers which enable you to adjust other layers that came before them. They contain all of the visual 'adjustments' meaning they do not add any content to the original photo; rather they are a sort of modification. This means that instead of adding a layer that is made up of content, you will be adding a layer of modification.

Adjustment layers are non-destructive. This means that they do not change the original content of the photo. A photo is comprised of pixels, and while most types of editing is implemented on to the original image, Photoshop and other specialized editing software add layers of modification on top of the original image. This preserves the original image under all of the layers in the way that if you were to strip them away, the image would come out virtually unchanged.

Adjustment layers can help you alter various features of the image, such as the brightness and the saturation. And while it may look like the photo itself is being manipulated, it is actually a transparent layer with the chosen modification on it, which is being displayed on top of the image.

How to Create Layers

The **Layers** tool has its own panel that lets you create, edit and view layers. You can find this panel on the bottom-right corner of the interface. Another way to access the tool is the **Window** option at the very top of the screen.

Creating Adjustment Layers

For new users, it is always better to start with adjustment layers. This is because of the non-destructive nature of adjustment layers, which can allow you to turn the layer's effects on and off to see how the pictures look with and without the layer.

1. Begin by downloading a sample image that has multiple layers; preferably one that is simple and with high contrast.
2. In the **Layers** panel, you will be able to see all the layers that are already on the original image.
3. Select any one of those layers by clicking on it. There will be a button named **Adjustment** towards the end of the **Layers** panel. This will then show a list of the adjustments you can make to the photo, via the adjustment layer.
4. Once you have selected the adjustment, for example **Hue/Saturation**, the **Properties** panel will open. This lets you customize the adjustment to your liking. You can also use the given buttons inside the panel to add adjustment layers.

Adjustment layers themselves are a very important part of Photoshop, and will be used throughout the guide.

Understanding Color, Levels and Curves

How to adjust the colors in your images, how to modify tonal ranges, how to fix dullness with color saturation, as well as understanding the Auto-Adjustment tool.

The images that you capture are bound to be faulty at some level. This is due to the vast potential for human error as well as technological limitations. Fortunately, you can perfect the images to some extent, and fix some of the common problems (Images that are too bright, too dark, too dull etc.).

These elements deal with essential editing, where visible aspects of the picture are manipulated and corrected. There are a multitude of corrections that you can do using **Color, Levels and Curves**. Here we will be looking at 3 specific corrections, namely **Saturation/Color**, **Levels**, **Curves**, as well as **Auto-Adjustment**.

Saturation

This is a form of color correction, where in case the image lacks vibrancy and the colors appear a bit too dull or suppressed, you can improve the vividness of the image by making the colors brighter and richer.

Alternately, you can make the colors less vivid, to the point of being completely colorless or in grayscale.

1. Start by adding a **Hue/Saturation** layer. Note that this will be an adjustment layer, and you may go back to the original image at any time.
2. A properties panel will have popped up, containing a slider for the saturation.
3. Drag the pointer left or right to adjust the saturation to your liking. Dragging it left will decrease saturation while dragging right will increase it.

It is important to note that excessive saturation can make the image look too vivid and therefore, unnatural. Sometimes, too much saturation can make the picture noisy and pixilated. This is especially true in the case of portraits, where the skin tone can come out unflattering.

Levels

Each image that you click is a mix of highlights, shadows and midtones. Highlights and shadows are the lightest and the darkest areas of the photo while midtones are the middle ground. When you are using the **Levels** element, you are actually modifying these very tones. **Contrast** and **Brightness** can also be used to this effect but both are not as efficient and powerful.

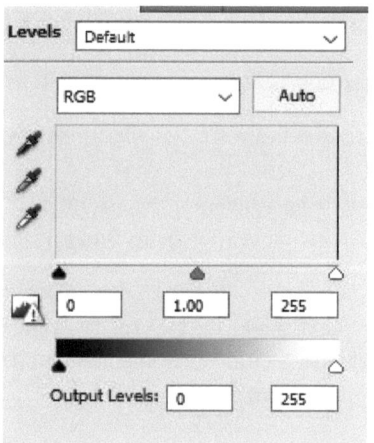

- Open the **Layers** tool and click on the **Levels** option.
- Next, open the tool's properties. There you will see a graph, directly in the centre. We call this graph a **Histogram**, and it displays details regarding the tones, highlights and shadows. If there is a blank gap in the middle or to a side of the histogram, it means the photo is underexposed.
- There will be 3 sliders directly below the histogram. These control the **Input Levels.** There will be another 2 sliders below these 3. These control the **Output Levels** and they are not to be used.
- If the image is underexposed, the light/white slider must be dragged to the left, till it reaches the histogram's edge. Sliding past this point and into the histogram will result in what is called **Clipping**. This takes away the detail in the image.
- In the opposite scenario, when the image is overexposed, you can slide the dark/black slider to the right.
- If despite all of this, the image is still too bright or too dark, you can adjust the tones with the gray slider.

In case you are using more than one adjustment layers, you will have to make the changes on each layer separately. You can always turn the adjustment layers off if you want to see the difference between the original and the edited image.

Curves

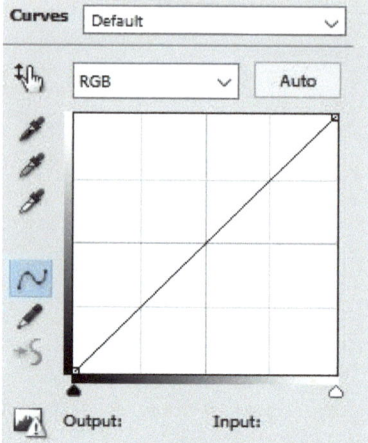

You can think of the **Curves** tool as a slightly more advanced version of **Levels**, in the way that it gives the user more control over the tonal range, as compared to **Levels**. This, while making it an extremely useful tool, also makes it slightly more complicated, which is why extra care should be taken when using it to edit photos.

Following are some of the more common adjustments that can be made, using the **Curves** tool.

Increasing Contrast: This is one of the simpler adjustments that the **Curves** tool can be used for.

- To make this adjustment, open up the **Curves** option. There will be a histogram in the window with a diagonal line running through it. This line is what is used to make the adjustment itself.
- Dragging the lower half of the diagonal line into the shadows will make them go darker.
- Dragging the upper half of the line out into the highlights will make them go brighter.

Decreasing Contrast: In images that are already quite contrasted in shadows and highlights, it is better to decrease contrast to a point.

- Dragging the curve line up into the shadows lightens them up. Be careful not to overdo this as excessively bright shadows look unrealistic.
- Dragging the curve line down in to the highlights section will darken them. Again, do not overdo this as it takes away from the realistic look of the photo.

Adjusting Curves: To adjust the curves, follow the steps given below.

- Open the layers menu and select **Curves**. This will open a new adjustment layer.
- Inside the properties panel, click on the line. This will create a point on to the line which can then be dragged to make adjustments.

- Click on the point and drag it to make adjustments to the curve.

As mentioned earlier, the **Curves** tool is not something that you should use until you have some editing experience. However, if you still wish to experience the workings of the tool, it is better to opt for one of the **Presets** that are available to the user. These will give you an idea how the tool works, while negating the need for any lengthy manual adjustments.

Noise Reduction and Image Sharpening

Adobe Photoshop possesses several features that allow the user to correct and clarify their images. This is highly beneficial for the photographer, as it allows them to adjust images which lack a certain amount of detail, or are excessively grainy and pixilated.

As you know, especially advanced DSLRs, are prone to adjusting images even when they don't necessarily need adjustment. Some of these adjustments are regarding the amount of noise, or at the opposite end, softness that an image ends up having.

There are different variable that go into each condition. Increasing the ISO of the camera will brighten the image but make it grainier, while not focusing correctly will make the images softer, and less detailed.

It is important to note that these too are tools that, if overused, will potentially ruin an image. However, if used correctly, after some practice, you will find that they yield brilliant results.

Let us start first with **Noise Reduction**.

Noise Reduction

Sometimes, when you click an image, it ends up looking too grainy and therefore, unattractive. In fact, there are few things more unattractive than a tasteless grainy image; especially one that should have had vibrant colors. To tackle this issue, you can use the **Noise Reduction** function within Photoshop. Before moving on to how it's done, it is important to first understand how the feature works.

When you apply the noise reduction feature on to an image, you essentially take away some of the information from within the image. This can be explained easily by thinking of each pixel as a piece of information. When these pixels are clearly visible on the image, the phenomenon is called **Noise**. Taking away some of these pixels can even out the arrangement, thus making the image look smoother and softer. However, too much information withdrawal can make the images look less detailed and blurred.

It is important to keep a highly observant eye on the changes that are occurring in the image as you are reducing noise. A good way to do this is to make tiny, gradual adjustments and work your way to a smoother and clearer image slowly.

Additionally, there are a multitude of different settings that you can control, such as **Strength**, **Preserve Details**, **Reduce Color Noise**, and **Sharpen Details**.

Strength: This setting dictates the level of noise reduction the image will be subjected to. The maximum value of **10** is recommended for starters, just so they can see the difference in the image that the tool is implementing. This level will also make it easier for you to see exactly how much of an effect the other settings have on the image.

Preserve Details: Another useful setting, this dictates how much of the original image detail will be saved. Using a value which is very low can cause the loss of image detail. On the other end, very high a level and you risk cancelling out the rest of the noise reduction effects.

Reduce Color Noise: Noise can sometimes occur in the form of colored patches in the image. This is referred to as color noise. The **Reduce Color Noise** setting can take care of this for you. However, too high a setting will result in the colors of the image bleeding together

Sharpen Details: When you reduce the color noise, you inevitably lose some of the detail. The sharpen details setting will allow you to return some of the detail back to the image. This can however, if done excessively, make the image grainy and noisy.

- To apply **Noise Reduction**, right-click on your preferred layer. From there, choose **Duplicate Layer**, which will let you make test adjustment without impacting the original image.
- Select this duplicate layer and open the **Filter** menu.
- Select the **Noise** option, and from the noise menu, select **Reduce Noise**.
- This will open a dialog box containing all 4 of the settings, which you can then adjust according to the function of each.
- You can see the effects by clicking on the **Preview** window, toggling it off and on. You can drag the preview window to any part of the image to see the results on that part.

- Click **OK** to apply the noise reduction.

Now let us move on to **Sharpening**.

Image Sharpening

Sharpening can cause a dull and less detailed image to look somewhat crisper and better defined. This is a useful feature as images often appear too dull of lacking of detail. This is especially true for images that have a lot of tonal variation.

A very common and effective way to sharpen the mage is to apply an **Unsharp Mask** filter. This tool has a few different settings that you can adjust as well. They are as follows.

Amount: Just as with the Strength setting, **Amount** dictates exactly how much of the sharpening is being applied on to the image.

Radius: This dictates the detail size that is to be adjusted. Using quite a low level for this setting will be better at this stage. For the majority of images, a radius of **0.3-0.5** is recommended. For images with higher resolution, you can use a higher radius.

Threshold: This setting tells the software to ignore or overlook some sections of the image when applying sharpening. While this can reduce some of the visible image noise, it can also cause some parts of the photo to remain as they were.

- To start, select your preferred layer and create a duplicate layer.
- This will cause a dialog box to open, in which you can name the layer for future reference.
- On this duplicate layer, open the **Filter** menu and select the **Sharpen** option.
- In the second menu that opens, choose **Unsharp Mask**.
- This will open another dialog box in which you can adjust the 3 settings discussed above, to your liking.
- Once again, you can view the effects in the preview window. Click on **OK** to apply the mask.

Photoshop Intermediate: Doing More to Your Images

Now, let us move on to some of the more intermediate tools and techniques. These techniques should not be delved into if you have not learned the basics of the software, as they contain some very nuanced and precise editing that can be potentially confusing for the first time editor.

Additional Layer Application

As we learned before, the **Layer** tool is quite expansive and versatile, and can be used in a variety of ways other than the basic adjustments. Here we will look at some additional, more advanced ways to use **Layers**.

Layer Opacity

Each layer that you make over an image can have its opacity adjusted. This decides how much transparency or opacity the layer will have, or how visible the layers below it will be.

- To begin, choose the layer on which you want to adjust opacity.
- On the top of the **Layers** panel, there will be the **Opacity** option which will have a drop-down button.
- There will appear a slider which you can drag from left to right, to adjust the layer opacity. If the opacity is set to the lowest level, the layer will become completely invisible.

Background Transparency

Photoshop, by default, uses a background layer for the majority of documents. The opacity and visibility of a background layer cannot be altered. There will be some occasions when you will want to alter the background layer and make it transparent. This can be done by hiding each layer except the one you want to show up front. There will appear a checkered pattern behind that specific layer, which indicates that the background layer is not visible.

Dodge and Burn

Dodge and **Burn**, as tools, are tried and tested techniques that have been borrowed from the era of film photography. These 2 tools are used to lighten or darken specific areas of an image, and are used to accentuate the already captured lights and shadows, in a non-destructive fashion. Conveniently, both tools work in the same way and the following guide can be used for both.

- Begin by creating a new layer
- Open the **Edit** button at the top of the interface, and choose fill.
- From here, you can choose the amount of gray that you can fill the layer in. Set the level at 50 percent gray.
- Select either the **Dodge** tool or the **Burn** tool
- Select the tip of the brush that you want to use on the image.
- There will open an options bar, in which you can select the range of the application.
- Now, you can drag the brush over the section of the photo that you want to either **Dodge** or **Burn**.

Layer Masks

Sometimes when editing, you may want only a particular section of a layer to be visible. For example, you may wish to remove a background from layers, so that the layer underneath it may show through. **Layer Masks** let you do this in a non-destructive manner.

Let us first start with creating a **Layer Mask**.

- Start by choosing a layer and clicking on the **Layer Mask** button at the base of the panel.
- A **Layer Mask,** in the shape of a white colored thumbnail, right beside the layer icon. You can edit the layer mask using a **Brush** tool.

Now, let us move on to editing a **Layer Mask**.

- Start by selecting the thumbnail for the layer mask.
- Next, open the **Brush** tool, and set the color of the foreground to white.
- Click on the areas of the layers and drag, to reveal the areas of the layer.
- Now, set the color of the foreground to black and drag the brush in the same way. This will hide the areas over which the brush has been dragged.
- Continue dragging the brush tool as desired.

Brushes

The **Brush** tool basically works as a real paintbrush, in the way that it lets you 'paint' on a layer. You have a multitude of brush settings at your disposal, making this one of the most versatile tools in the entire software.

What makes the **Brush** tool even more special is the fact that it is used every time there is a need to implement an adjustment on certain areas of the image with precision. Aside from the **Eraser** tool, no other tool lets you do this.

You can also customize the brush that you will be using, as well as create your own brushes. At present, there are thousands of user-created brushes available for free as well as for purchase.

- To start using the **Brush** tool, select the tool from the panel, and use the click-and-drag motion to start painting on the image. The **B** on a keyboard serves as a shortcut, letting you access the tool quickly.
- You can also use the **Color Picker** tool to select different brush colors.

Following are some of the settings that you can change, to alter the effect of the brush.

Size: If you wish to change the brush's size, click on **Brush Picker**. This will open a drop down box in which you can adjust the size of the brush.

Hardness: This setting is used to change the hardness of the brush around the edges. The very same box where you adjusted the size of the brush also has a slider that lets you adjust the hardness. Setting it to a halfway point is the best option, as it will soften the edges of the brush, making the strokes seem more natural and less obvious.

Brush Tip: The same menu that was used for the previous settings also contains a variety of **Brush** tip options. These let you implement a unique effect on the image, sometimes even mimicking real-life drawing tools.

Brush Opacity: You can alter the brush opacity as well, from the top panel, right beside the **Mode**. The default opacity of brushes is 100 percent however this can be changed to make the strokes more translucent.

Photoshop Advanced: Editing Like a Pro

Having covered some of the basic as well as intermediate editing techniques, we now move on to some of the more advanced image manipulation options. As we have learned early on in the book, Photoshop is incredibly diverse and expansive, in the way that it gives the user an astounding array of options, letting them make countless different changes to the images.

Following are some advanced Photoshop procedures that you can touch upon, once you have mastered the software at the fundamental and intermediate level.

Raw Images

The **RAW** image option in most digital SLR cameras lets you record a significant amount of additional detail, as compared to the standard JPEG. Simply put, you are recording the scene in front of you as it is, without the machine implementing any effects or space saving tricks on it.

It is quite similar to a strip of film that has not been edited in the darkroom. There are minimal to no changes made to the image, and it retains almost all of its integrity.

Editing RAW images can be quite rewarding, once you take into account all the control you are given with your editing choices. However, it is included in the advanced techniques as it is also quite complicated for the new editor.

Adobe Camera Raw

The Adobe Camera RAW software is designed as a RAW image focused extension of popular photo editing software such as Photoshop, Lightroom, Photoshop Elements and Adobe Bridge. It is quite similar, at the basic build level, to Lightroom, as both are built upon the same processing technology.

Almost all major camera brands are supported by the software. Additionally, it also supports the **Digital Negative (DNG)** format.

Here you will learn how to edit RAW images using the Adobe Camera Raw software. If you have the latest version of Photoshop or Lightroom, this software should come as standard, embedded into the editing software. Once you have determined that it is indeed installed and updated, you are ready to edit RAW images on Photoshop using Adobe Camera Raw.

Following are some of the more common as well as useful edits that you can do on RAW images.

Selecting the Channel
- Start by opening the RAW file on Camera RAW.
- At the base of the interface, there will be the channel selector, set at a default 8-Bit. This option will be available in the form of either a popup window or drop-down menu.
- From that menu, select the **16-Bit** option. This gives you significantly more flexibility when editing.

Adjusting the White Balance

- Towards the right of the interface, there will be a sidebar with a variety of sliders.
- The first 2 sliders are used to adjust the White Balance of the Image. White balance can be altered in the camera itself; however in the case that you need to adjust the white balance later on, this option will help you do so.
- You can also select a preset inside the drop-down menu, as well as change the tint and/or temperature of the image .

Adjusting Exposure

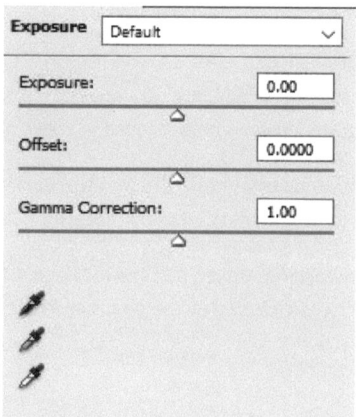

Adjusting the exposure of an image is much easier to do with RAW files.

- There will be a histogram on the right side, which you can use to decide how much variation is needed.
- The slider named **Exposure** will let you adjust the overall exposure of the image.
- The slider named **Recovery** will help you in recovering the details that have been lost in the highlights.
- The slider named **Fill Light** will allow you to fill the shadows, as the name suggests.
- It is important to try moving each slider and seeing how it affects the image. To undo each adjustment, you can settle the slider back where it originally was.

Adjusting Contrast

Directly beneath the sliders that adjust the exposure, are the contrast sliders. These will allow you to change how the contrast of an image appears. These particular sliders are very effective in letting some of the image's detail and texture emerge fully.

- The slider named **Contrast** allows you to alter the overall contrast of the photo. This is done in both highlights as well as shadows.
- The black colored slider will let you darken the black areas of an image.

- The light colored slider will brighten the image's highlights.
- The mid tones can be adjusted using the slider named **Clarity**.

Adjusting Color

Directly beneath **Clarity**, you will find the **Saturation** and **Vibrance** sliders. These will allow you to adjust the vividness of the color in the image, making it either more lush or muted. **Vibrance** makes the colors that are less pronounced, stand out. While **Saturation** makes the more visible colors deeper and more 'saturated'. It is important to not overdo this feature as it makes the image look artificially processed.

Opening the Image

Once you have completed the editing, click on the **Open** button to load the image on to Photoshop. This will additionally allow you to retain all of the edits, each time you open the image in Photoshop. From here, you can make additional edits using the options given by Photoshop.

About the Author

Ryan Crane learned about photography by performing extensive research and then applying the learned principles in the field over a number of years. He is now a well renowned photographer and wants to help others become better at photography as well. He believes that you can become a better photographer, if you can work on your skills and follow the best advices that are on offer in the digital world.

One of the best sources in this regards is the http://improveyourphotographyonline.com/ website which allows you to learn through tutorials and different sessions.

Ryan tries to help inspiring photographers by providing them with a number of image resources such as backgrounds and tutorials. His work is available at http://www.ryancranephotography.com/ and can be viewed by any budding photographer.